HAL•LEONARD®
VIOLIN PLAY-ALONG

AUDIO ACCESS INCLUDED

LINDSEY STIRLING
SELECTIONS FROM
WARMER IN THE WINTER

T0039570

PLAYBACK+
Speed • Pitch • Balance • Loop

To access audio visit:
www.halleonard.com/mylibrary

Enter Code
1552-0571-5054-1481

ISBN 978-1-5400-1465-8

HAL•LEONARD®
7777 W. BLUEMOUND RD. P.O. BOX 13819 MILWAUKEE, WI 53213

Jon Vriesacker, violin
Audio arrangements by Peter Deneff
Recorded and Produced by Jake Johnson at Paradyme Productions

Warmer in the Winter

Words and Music by Lindsey Stirling, Evan Bogart and Brian Phillips

All I Want For Christmas is You

Words and Music by Mariah Carey and Walter Afanasieff
Arranged by Lindsey Stirling and Chris Walden

Christmas C'mon

Words and Music by Lindsey Stirling, Jon Levine and Autumn Rowe

Jingle Bell Rock

Words and Music by Joe Beal and Jim Boothe
Arranged by Lindsey Stirling and Chris Walden

Let It Snow! Let It Snow! Let It Snow!

Words by Sammy Cahn
Music by Jule Styne
Arranged by Lindsey Stirling and Chris Walden

11

Time to Fall in Love

Words and Music by Lindsey Stirling, Jordan Witzigreuter and Cameron Alexander Walker-Wright

We Three Gentlemen

"We Three Kings" by John Hopkins, Jr., "God Rest Ye Merry, Gentlemen" Traditional English
and "Ukrainian Bell Carol" by Mykola Leontovych
Arranged by Lindsey Stirling

You're a Mean One, Mr. Grinch

Lyrics by Dr. Seuss
Music by Albert Hague
Arranged by Lindsey Stirling, Chris Walden and Ely Rise

Christmas C'mon

Words and Music by Lindsey Stirling, Jon Levine and Autumn Rowe

Time to Fall in Love

Words and Music by Lindsey Stirling, Jordan Witzigreuter and Cameron Alexander Walker-Wright

In the town, bus-y peo-ple all a-round, mov-in' to those sleigh - bell sounds. Mmm, yeah. We can drive in this one horse-pow-ered ride. And I hope that will be all right. Mmm, yeah. If the sum- -mer is a five or a six then the white win-ter weath-er makes the

D.S. al Coda   **CODA**   **16**

top of my list

Christ-mas is the time to fall in love. The time to fall in love Ev-'ry-bod-y's look-ing for some-one. ev-'ry-bod-y's look-ing for some-one. The sug-ar-plum sweet-heart mis-tle-toe scene; all the girls are shop-ping and they're look-ing for me. 'Cause Christ-mas is the time to fall in love, the time to fall in love.

Warmer in the Winter

Words and Music by Lindsey Stirling, Evan Bogart and Brian Phillips

Last year I was on my own, _ hi-ber-nat-in' in my em-pty home. _

San-ta did-n't e-ven help. _ I left a plate of coo-kies but I ate 'em my-self. _

This _ year feels so brand new. _ Tie a rib-bon 'round me and you. _

San-ta is __ check-in' twice, _ he's try-in' to fig-ure out if you've been naugh-ty or nice. _ Roads are

closed. Snow is fal-ling. _ But I don't __ real-ly mind.

I know that it's cold out-side. _ The world __ is bun-dled up in white. _

I just need you by my side, _ 'cause I'm warm-er in the win-ter with you. __ Woo!

I know that it's cold out-side, _ the world is bun-dled

up in white. _ I just need you by my side. _ 'Cause I'm warm-er in the win-ter with you. _

__ Yeah. _ The tem-p'ra-ture is toast-y for two. Oh, oh, __ I'm warm-er in the win-ter with you.

You're a Mean One, Mr. Grinch

Lyrics by Dr. Seuss
Music by Albert Hague
Arranged by Lindsey Stirling, Chris Walden and Ely Rise